Coloring f

A Mini Mandala

Susanne F. Fincher

Shambhala
Boulder
2016

Shambhala Publications, Inc.
4720 Walnut Street
Boulder, Colorado 80301
www.shambhala.com

© 2013 by Susanne F. Fincher
Introduction © 2016 by Susanne F. Fincher

This book is a slightly revised edition of *Coloring Mandalas 4* (Shambhala, 2013).

9 8 7 6 5 4 3 2 1

Printed in Canada

♾This edition is printed on acid-free paper that meets the
American National Standards Institute Z39.48 Standard.
♻Shambhala Publications makes every effort to print on recycled paper.
For more information please visit www.shambhala.com.
Distributed in the United States by Penguin Random House LLC
and in Canada by Random House of Canada Ltd

ISBN 978-1-61180-424-9

Introduction

Driving the flat open roads of West Texas one summer day, it seemed that I was at the center of a vast circular space covered with tough, dry grass and mesquite brush. My gaze traveled into the distance, where the horizon looked like the rim of a fry pan, marking the edge of the earth in every direction. Feeling the urge for a better look, I pulled over, got out of the car, and made my way through the brush to a sandy patch nearby. The sun burned down from the center of a clear blue sky that held nothing back. The intense light forced my eyes into narrow slits. I was alone.

Slowly I turned, surveying the empty land while the wind whipped my skirt. I saw that I was at the center of the earth. Overwhelmed by the vast space, I started to panic. Then I remembered the sun. I was not alone after all. Suddenly inspired, I picked up a piece of white caliche rock and scraped a circle in the crusty sand around the place where I stood. Standing tall at the center of my circle, I felt secure, anchored, protected. I felt kinship with the land, the sky, the sun. I had joined the vast cosmic forces at play on these arid high plains. Like many before me at such times, I had constructed a *mandala* to bring the moment into focus, manage the energy it stirred, and draw the event into a pattern I could understand.

Mandalas (Sanskrit for "sacred circles") are circles that set aside a time or place as special. Mandalas have been constructed since ancient times by human beings the world over. The desire to create a mandala can arise spontaneously, as I discovered on that drive through West Texas. Coloring mandalas like the ones in this book is a modern way to experience this ancient human tradition.

THE MEANING OF MANDALAS

Many of the mandalas in this book are inspired by some of the oldest art in the world. These early mandalas were simply circles with a dot in the center that probably symbolizes the sun high in the sky. Others are circles with lines that cross at the center, dividing the circle into four equal parts. This pattern of four may connote the four cardinal directions, the four seasons, or even the front, back, and sides of the human body. The number four is especially significant in mandalas of orientation and relates to knowing oneself and one's place: of *being*, one of the themes of this book.

Sometimes we see a mandala with a four-armed cross that has grown "feet," revealing the ancient belief that the sun *walked* across the sky. This lively design conveys a sense that the arms of the cross are turning around the center of the circle. As Jill Purce notes, "All images which prescribe these movements are essentially mandalic, centering and ordering, because, on whatever level, the movement is echoing the cosmic movement of which it is symbolic."

Sadly, the ancient walking sun motif, or swastika (Sanskrit for "auspicious") was co-opted by the German Nazi party in the 1930s and continues to carry a dark and sinister meaning in Western countries. Our inclusion of the swastika in some of the mandalas in this book is an effort to reclaim for Westerners the older positive meaning the swastika enjoys in Eastern and Native American traditions.

In addition to mandalas based on the number four, a great many mandalas are based on the number five. This number is significant as a symbol of the human body. Two arms, two legs, and a head add up to five. Mandalas of five-pointed stars, pentagons—and swastikas with a pronounced center—can suggest a human body in motion or *doing*, the second theme of this book.

MANDALAS AS PERSONAL EXPRESSION

The desire to express oneself by drawing circles is apparently quite natural. Kindergartners create pure, simple mandalas that reflect their awareness of themselves and their surroundings. Mandalas come about in children's art at a particular developmental stage. Kids begin with random scribbles during infancy, and by about age three they are creating circles, suns, and crosses very similar to the art of ancient peoples. They go on to produce circles with the features of a human face and with lines suggesting arms and legs connected to the circle. The child's drawing of mandalas may well support her development of body image along with the discovery of herself as a unique being capable of willed action. These initial discoveries form the core identity of a person.

As we grow up, adults who create mandalas are perhaps unconsciously invoking their core identity in a process that is both retrospective and prospective, that is, looking within to the center point of self, established early in life, and then formulating a new circle of self from this center in order to take action in the world. As psychologist Rudolf Arnheim has pointed out, the centered circle is a fitting metaphor for the task of being human: "The spread of action from the generating core of the self."

Mandalas can also be viewed as reflections of psychological processes, as the Swiss psychiatrist Carl G. Jung proposed. According to Jung, the psyche includes both conscious and unconscious elements. He agreed with his contemporary the American psychologist William James that a person could not, at any given moment, be aware of the entire contents of the psyche. *Consciousness*, including personal identity, consists only of that which is "present to the thought at any time," as James wrote.

The center of consciousness is self-awareness, which Jung called *ego*. Information that is forgotten, not yet realized, or deeply embedded in the body's physicality Jung understood to be in the *personal unconscious*. He also posited a deep stratum of the psyche derived from shared human history that he dubbed the *collective unconscious*. The collective unconscious is the repository of natural ordering potentials accrued over thousands of years of human experience. Jung called these potentials *archetypes*.

One of the archetypes Jung discovered functions as a natural centering and organizing principle for the whole psyche, even though it resides deep in the unconscious. This center, which Jung called the *Self*, to distinguish it from the ego, provides the matrix for development of the ego and motivates a lifelong striving toward wholeness. The Self is also the generating force behind mandalas.

Jung found from his own experience as well as his patients' that creating mandalas can help contain, process, and integrate information during psychological growth. He noted that creating mandalas provides a stabilizing anchor for individuals. Jung considered the appearance of mandalas in patients' artwork as evidence that they were growing toward fulfilling their unique pattern of wholeness.

The American art therapist Joan Kellogg incorporated the mandala designs Jung identified into her own theory of mandalas and personal growth, the Archetypal Stages of the Great Round of Mandala (hereafter referred to as the *Great Round*). Kellogg identified mandalas associated with twelve stages of human growth and development. Twelve is a number rich in historical, religious, and numerological meaning: twelve months of the year, twelve signs of the zodiac, twelve tribes of Israel, twelve apostles of Jesus, and twelve links of dependent arising in the Buddhist Wheel of Life. A geometric figure with twelve sides, a dodecagon, is very much like a circle. For this reason, J. E. Cirlot concludes, "systems or patterns based upon the circle or the cycle tend to have twelve as the end-limit." So it is no surprise that Kellogg arranged the stages and mandalas associated with her system in a circular configuration.

Each stage of the Great Round is characterized by a quality of consciousness, a view of reality, and particular tasks, challenges, or concerns. Individuals

Archetypal Stages of the Great Round of Mandala.
(Kellogg 1978; drawn by Susanne Fincher 2003)

are thought to repeat the cycle often as they grow and change during their lives. The twelve stages are called the Void, Bliss, Labyrinth/Spiral, Beginning, Target, Paradoxical Split/Dragon Fight, Squaring the Circle, Functioning in the World, Crystallization, Gates of Death, Fragmentation, and Transcendent Ecstasy. In this book we focus on mandalas of two stages of the Great Round: Stage Seven, *Squaring the Circle*, and Stage Eight, *Functioning in the World*.

Stage Seven is a place of balance, integration, and self-realization. It is associated with *being*. The term *squaring the circle* comes from a geometric conundrum that baffled ancient thinkers. So it is that the design of a square touching a circle suggests the achievement of perfect balance between the known and

Figure 1. Mandala representing Stage Seven of the Great Round: Squaring the Circle.

the unknowable (see Figure 1). For Jung this signified the yoking of the *ego* (known) and the *Self* (unknowable), the ultimate goal of psychological development. This balance is mediated by the mandalas of Stage Seven, Squaring the Circle, and similar designs that indicate "the premonition of a centre of personality, a kind of central point within the psyche, to which everything is related, by which everything is arranged, and which is itself a source of energy. The energy of the central point is manifested in the almost irresistible compulsion and urge to become what one is" (Jung, *Mandala Symbolism*, 73).

These mandalas express a special experience of *being*. They make a statement, and are sometimes reminiscent of the designs of heraldic shields carried as an

Figure 2. Mandala with a calm design.

emblem of personal power. Mandalas of Squaring the Circle usually have the structure of four within the circle. Some examples of such designs include Greek crosses, sun symbols like those in ancient mandalas, and squares inside or outside the mandala circle. Designs are usually symmetrical, have a strong center, and convey stability, balance, and substance (see Figure 2).

Stage Eight, Functioning in the World, is associated with energy, action, and doing. During Stage Eight qualities of creativity, ingenuity, teamwork, and productivity are prominent. You are at your most effective during Stage Eight on the Great Round, and your activities are valued in our culture. You often earn money for what you do while in Stage Eight, Functioning in the World.

Figure 3. Mandala Representing Stage Eight of the Great Round: Functioning in the World.

The mandalas associated with Functioning in the World frequently display a structure based on the number five, which is a traditional metaphor for the human body. Your arms and legs stretch out to claim your body's points of maximum extension in space. Your five-fingered hands allow you to take hold of and shape materials. Your five-toed feet support and balance your body so that you can move with confidence. Typical Stage Eight mandalas consist of five-pointed stars (see Figure 3), flowers with five petals, and centered swirls. Four-armed swastikas with a pronounced center providing the fifth element are also typical of Stage Eight.

The theme of *doing* associated with Stage Eight can also be found in mandalas that suggest movement with stimulating optical patterns. One of the gifts of

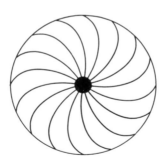

Figure 4. Mandala with a lively design.

human consciousness is the ability to imagine yourself in someone else's shoes. You experience this while watching a movie—when a character slips and falls, you flinch as if you were the one losing your balance. This is a form of empathy that also enables you to feel qualities of lines and patterns. Viewing a lively mandala design stimulates kinesthetic responses in your body (see Figure 4). Your energy naturally aligns with the quality of the lines in the mandala. When you add these kinesthetic responses to the physical movement you make when coloring mandalas, it is easy to see how you can become energized by coloring such designs.

Coloring the mandalas in this book allows you to interact with forms that evoke both steady, centered *being* and active, skillful *doing*. Perhaps coloring mandalas of Stage Seven, Squaring the Circle, will bring you the calm self-assurance associated with this stage of the Great Round. Adding colors to Stage Eight mandalas may increase your energy and help you take the next right step. Above all, coloring these designs will be a pleasurable affirmation of who you are. I hope that you find lots of enjoyment working with *Coloring for Insight*.

Susanne F. Fincher
Atlanta, Georgia
2016

REFERENCES

Arnheim, Rudolf. *The Power of the Center*. Berkeley and Los Angeles: University of California Press, 1988.

Cirlot, Juan Eduardo. *A Dictionary of Symbols*. Trans. Jack Sage. New York: Philosophical Library, 1962.

Fincher, Susanne F. *Creating Mandalas: For Insight, Healing, and Self-Expression*. Rev. ed. Boston: Shambhala Publications, 1991, 2010.

James, William. *The Varieties of Religious Experience: A Study of Human Nature*. London: Collier Macmillan Publishers, 1961.

Jung, Carl G. *Mandala Symbolism*. Princeton, N.J.: Princeton University Press, 1973.

———. *The Archetypes and the Collective Unconscious*, 2nd Edition. Trans. R. F. C. Hull. Princeton, N.J.: Princeton University Press, 1969.

Kellogg, Joan. *Mandala: Path of Beauty*. Rev. ed. Raleigh, N.C.: MARI Resources, 2002.

Purce, Jill. *The Mystic Spiral*. New York: Thames and Hudson, 1980.

MANDALAS FOR COLORING

Mandala 1

Being and doing in the world mean that your words and actions flow from who you really are.

Mandala 2

This mandala resembles a Celtic shield embellished with jewels and knot work. Its center suggests a compass rose. The mandala communicates stability, protection, and clear thinking.

Mandala 3

Intricate weaving suggests a soft square of knot work enclosing a Greek cross in the center space of this mandala. A strong sense of self can be expressed in gentle ways.

Mandala 4

Rhythmic arcs recalling magnetic energy add a sense of dynamic movement to this mandala of strong, simple lines. Inner *being* gives rise to radiant *doing*.

Mandala 5

Overlapping circles play in and around clear, lined squares: the convergence of *being* and *doing*.

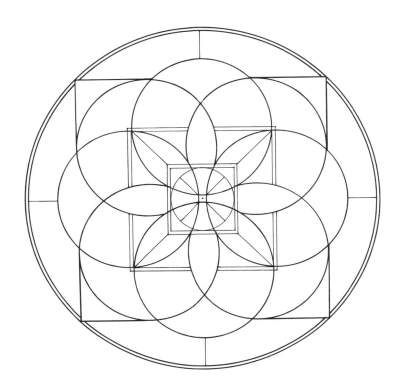

Mandala 6

Myriad patterns of four are layered in this mandala, conveying an intricate message about *being*.

Mandala 7

A tree symbolizes wholeness during a moment of self-reflection and cosmic connection.

Mandala 8

Wings shelter the complex generative pattern at the center of this mandala.

Mandala 9

This mandala is inspired by abstract tantric art of India. Which pathway to the center will your colors illuminate? There is no right or wrong way.

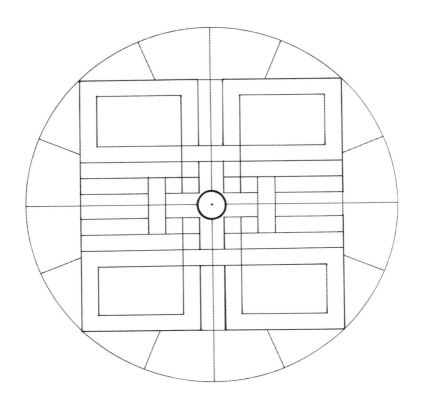

Mandala 10

The centers of four overlapping rings are the corners of an interior square poised in readiness to move: the shift from *being* to *doing*.

Mandala 11

The conundrum of Squaring the Circle is explored in this mandala with its rich array of lines and forms dancing in harmony.

Mandala 12

Convivial abundance is suggested by the exotic flowers, large and small, that bloom in a lively balance within this mandala.

Mandala 13

Flames illuminate the boundary of this mandala, suggesting the intensity of consciousness when *being* is focused.

Mandala 14

Like a modern version of a jewel-encrusted Byzantine cross, this mandala holds multiplicity in one powerful design: a statement of *being*.

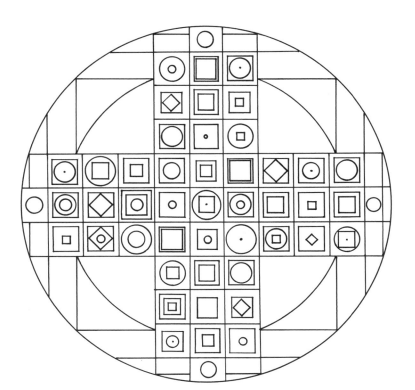

Mandala 15

The center pattern of this mandala is a hexagram developed in response to the query, what is the situation surrounding this mandala coloring book? The hexagram is called *Progress*. Alfred Huang notes, "Proceeding should be stable, gradual, and steady."

Mandala 16

A Crusader's cross marks the center of this mandala. Embarking on a quest is sometimes part of your personal journey as you experience Stage Seven, Squaring the Circle.

Mandala 17

The optical effect of movement is created by rhythmically layered circles generating an outer mandala boundary. The swirling circular paths converge and cross at the center, suggesting a hidden cross that appears to exert magnetic force. Another exploration of Squaring the Circle.

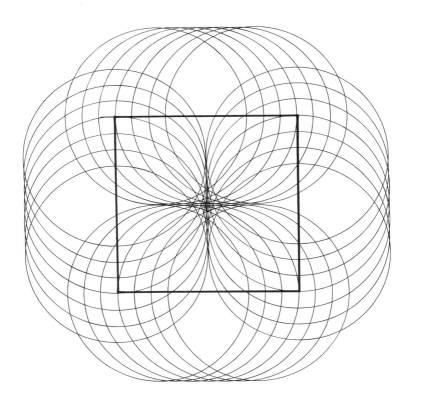

Mandala 18

Like a package tied with ribbon, this mandala hints at pleasant surprises to come.

Mandala 19

Tendrils unfurl as flowers in full bloom happily show their faces to the sun.

Mandala 20

A fiery circle encloses the centered Greek cross. Mysterious objects rest on the shoulders of the cross. Use your imagination to decide what they are, and know that it is your unconscious speaking to you.

Mandala 21

This mandala holds a map of the night sky. The center point is the North Star. Small squares are connected to represent the Big Dipper, which always points to the North Star. At the top is the Big Dipper's spring position. Moving counterclockwise, the position of the Big Dipper is shown during summer, fall, and winter.

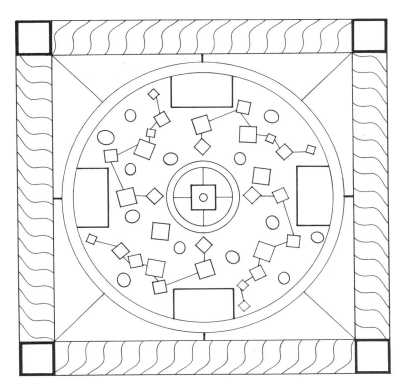

Mandala 22

The intertwining patterns of Celtic knot work enrich this depiction of a cross that could be carved from stone.

Mandala 23

Fiddlehead ferns flank the simple cross at the center of this mandala. They suggest the heightened energy that manifests as one moves into Stage Eight, Functioning in the World.

Mandala 24

This mandala could be a lunar calendar. The smaller circles near the edge of the mandala then would represent the twenty-eight days of a lunar month, or *moonth*. The four larger circles could represent the moon and her many phases. Radiance appears to stream outward from the central circle, which in our calendar represents the Sun.

Mandala 25

The inner circle gives the impression of being a magnifying lens, showing what is underneath in great detail. Such is the intense focus possible during Stage Seven, when sensing and thinking are highlighted.

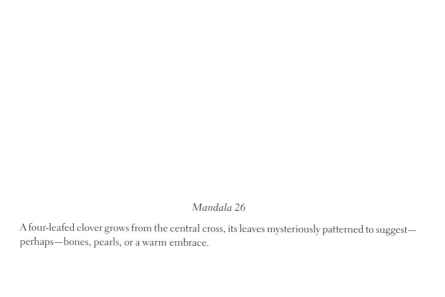

Mandala 26

A four-leafed clover grows from the central cross, its leaves mysteriously patterned to suggest—perhaps—bones, pearls, or a warm embrace.

Mandala 27

The dance of the opposites, as we see in this passionate tango, is highlighted during Stage Seven. Four phases in the circle of life are symbolized around the periphery, flowing from one into the other.

Mandala 28

Five flowers bring the energy of Stage Eight *doing* into a mandala with four tropical plants quietly spreading their leaves.

Mandala 29

A turning swastika of wings fills a square surrounded by lotus petals. This mandala suggests the energy of *doing* typical of Stage Eight, Functioning in the World.

Mandala 30

A four-armed cross is camouflaged in a dazzling design of interlocking waves.

Mandala 31

Ruffled petals create a many-layered flower that recalls the five points of the human body: head, arms and hands, legs and feet.

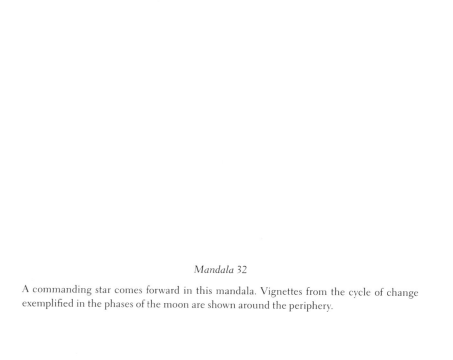

Mandala 32

A commanding star comes forward in this mandala. Vignettes from the cycle of change exemplified in the phases of the moon are shown around the periphery.

Mandala 33

Stage Eight, Functioning in the World, is a time of working skillfully with people, as suggested by the hand touching five smaller mandalas inside the large circle.

Mandala 34

The central star anchors circles that seem to spin with centrifugal force into varied configurations. This mandala is a lively depiction of the energy of *doing*.

Mandala 35

This mandala appears to celebrate the expanding energy generated by the stage called Functioning in the World.

Mandala 36

Rotating arms extending from a sturdy square appear to scoop in energy. Coloring this mandala perhaps will increase your energy for *doing*.

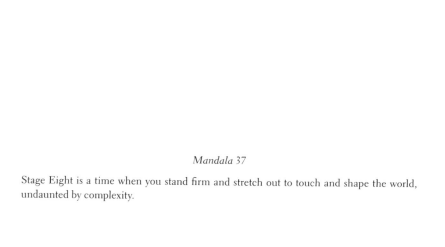

Mandala 37

Stage Eight is a time when you stand firm and stretch out to touch and shape the world, undaunted by complexity.

Mandala 38

Stage Eight invites the full expression of your talents, knowledge, and skills. You are the star of your own creations.

Mandala 39

This mandala appears a bit out of balance at first, but take another look. Five air-filled sails turn above a serene structure of four stylized petals. The layers are firmly attached to the center. This whimsical, yet grounded, mandala combines elements of both *being* and *doing*.

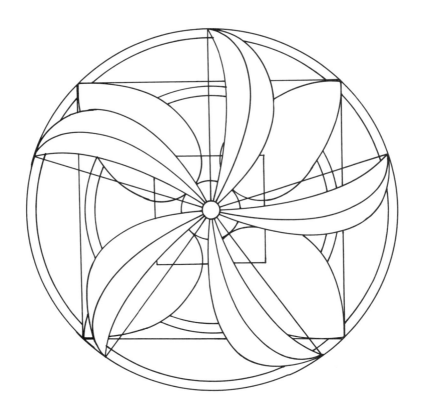

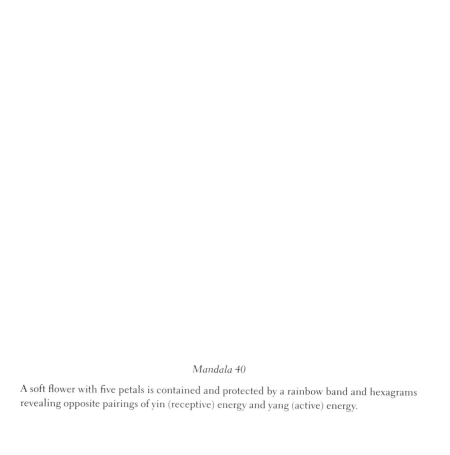

Mandala 40

A soft flower with five petals is contained and protected by a rainbow band and hexagrams revealing opposite pairings of yin (receptive) energy and yang (active) energy.

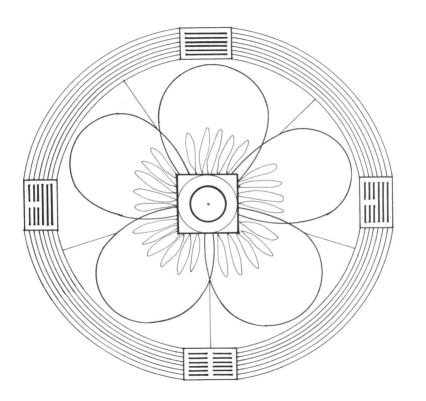

Mandala 41

This is a lively design with a rotating cross at the center. Four gateways near the boundary of the mandala could symbolize the four cardinal directions, spiritual guides, or aspects of a project you are doing.

Mandala 42

This design is inspired by traditional Eastern mandalas structured like a temple with four gates. The square recalls Stage Seven, Squaring the Circle, and *being*. The inner structure of five circles recalls Stage Eight, Functioning in the World, typified by active *doing*. Multiple lines flow through the mandala suggesting, perhaps, your varied experiences coloring the mandalas of the Great Round included in this book.

Create your own mandala design!

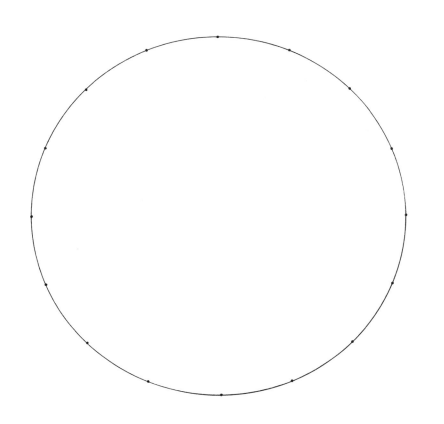

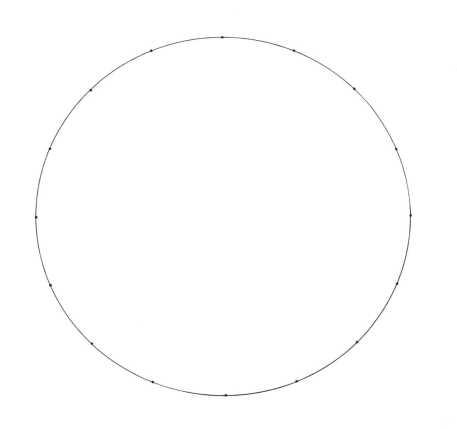

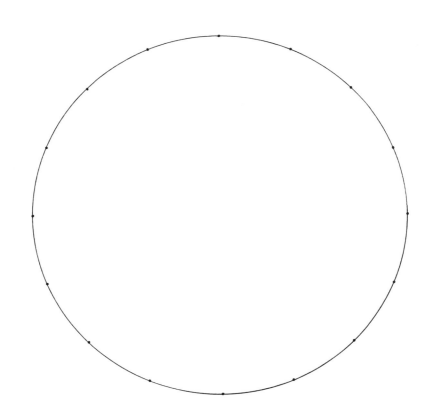

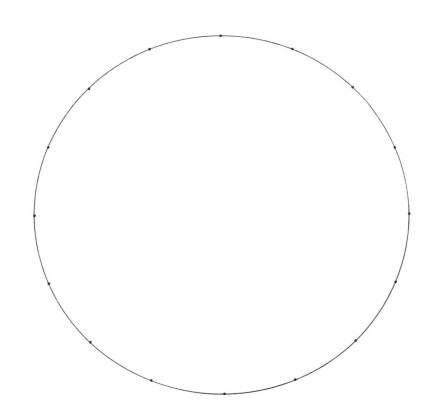

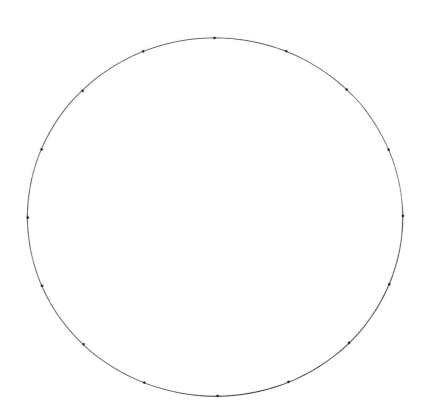